P9-CFP-533

Creative Ideas

Program Authors

Connie Juel, Ph.D.

Jeanne R. Paratore, Ed.D.

Deborah Simmons, Ph.D.

Sharon Vaughn, Ph.D.

Copyright © 2011 by Pearson Education, Inc., or its affiliates. All Rights Reserved. Printed in the United States of America. This publication is protected by copyright, and permission should be obtained from the publisher prior to any prohibited reproduction, storage in a retrieval system, or transmission in any form or by any means, electronic, mechanical, photocopying, recording, or likewise. For information regarding permissions, write to Pearson Curriculum Group Rights & Permissions, One Lake Street, Upper Saddle River, New Jersey 07458.

Pearson, Scott Foresman, and Pearson Scott Foresman are trademarks, in the U.S. and/or other countries, of Pearson Education, Inc., or its affiliates.

Glenview, Illinois
Boston, Massachusetts
Chandler, Arizona
Upper Saddle River, New Jersey

ISBN-13: 978-0-328-45276-7
ISBN-10:   0-328-45276-9

9 10 V011 14 13

Creative Ideas

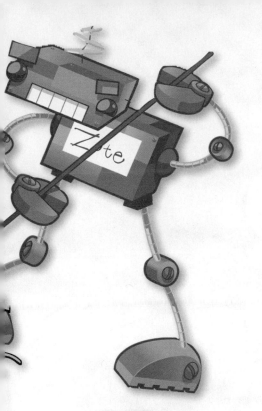

Contents

Ideas Become Inventions

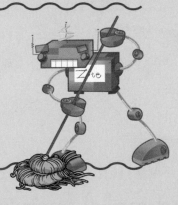
See page 27 for My New Words!

Ideas Become Inventions

What can you do with an idea? You can plan and make an invention! Inventions help us and make things fun. Some are huge, like jets. Some are not huge, like gum and notes that stick.

What is the sign of a good invention? This man had an idea. His name was Alexander Graham Bell. Alexander Graham Bell made this machine. It helped us. It let us chat with pals. Kids still use it to chat with pals.

Kids can make things too. A kid named Frank had a drink. It had a stick in it. Frank took his drink out of his house in winter and left it.

Time passed, and his drink froze with the stick in it. It was like an ice cube on a stick.

Frank had made a snack on a stick. Kids still like these snacks on sticks. Kids like grape ice snacks. Kids like lime ice snacks. Yum, yum!

Eve thinks and thinks. Then Eve plans and plans. Next, Eve takes tubes, tape, and wire to make an invention. Eve's best pal, Suze, will help Eve.

"We can use this at camp!" Suze tells Eve.
What do you think these best pals will make?
What can you make? What is the sign of a
good invention?

IN-LINE

It's lots and lots of fun to skate! Ice skates use long blades and zip fast on white ice. Kids can skate on places that aren't ice too. Then kids don't use skates with blades. These skates use wheels.

SKATES

by Carla Smith

This is an in-line skate. The idea for it came from Scott and Brennan Olson. The Olsons spotted an old, odd skate in a shop. It had wheels in a long line. This odd skate gave these men an idea.

Brennan Olson

Scott Olson

Back at their house, the Olsons took blades off ice skates. They added a long line of wheels on one skate and then on the other. Next, the men added brakes to help the skates stop.

brake

These skates went fast. And brakes helped make them safe. Little kids liked them. Big kids liked them. Moms and dads liked them!

The men grinned, "We can make lots of in-line skates and sell them!"

The men got a machine that helped them make in-line skates. They made the skates at home. People kept asking for skates. The men had to hire help. The big sales of in-line skates are a sign that these men did a good job.

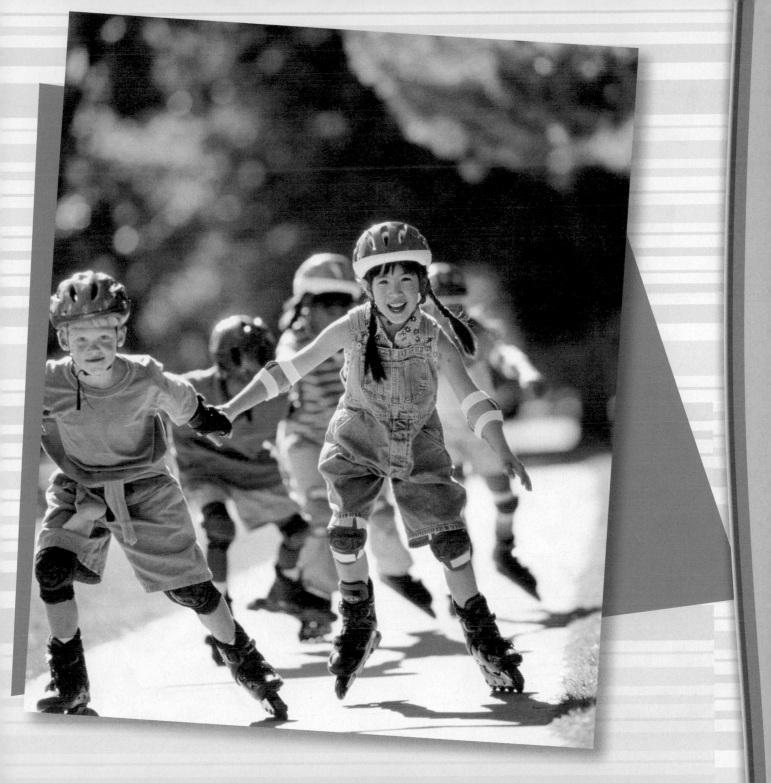

Lots and lots of kids like skating on these fun skates. It's nice that these men had this fine idea!

ZUTE

by Dennis Franklin
illustrated by Bill McGuire

Jade and Luke got tubes, wires, and pipes. They tapped and banged. They made a huge machine. They made Zute. See the sign on it?

Jade and Luke like Zute. They hope Zute can help. If Zute can, Mom and Dad will like Zute too.

Zute will help Jade and Luke a bit. But Zute
won't help them a lot. Zute can't.

Zute will make beds. But Zute won't make
beds well. Zute can't. This bed is still a mess.
This is the best Zute can do.

Zute will mop the house. But it won't mop well. It can't. Zute spills the water.

This is the best Zute can do.

Mom and Dad don't like beds that aren't made well. Mom and Dad don't like spilled water.

What do Mom and Dad think about Zute?
Mom and Dad don't think Zute helps. Zute
can't make beds well. Zute can't mop well. And
Mom and Dad think Zute is just too big. Zute is
cute, but it will smash things. Zute can't help it.

Mom and Dad don't think that Zute can live in the house. What can Jade and Luke do?

Jade has an idea. "Let's fix Zute!" Jade tells Luke.

Jade and Luke take pipes away from Zute. Now Zute isn't so huge. Next, Jade and Luke add tubes and wires. These tubes and wires will help Zute.

Now Zute can do a new thing. What is it? Will Mom and Dad like it?

Zute will not make beds. Zute will not mop. Zute will make tunes! Zute's tunes make Jade and Luke smile. Zute's tunes make Mom and Dad smile too. They think its tunes are nice.

Mom and Dad like Zute. Jade and Luke like
Zute a lot! Zute is glad. Zute gives Jade and Luke
a big hug!

A Time Line of Fun!

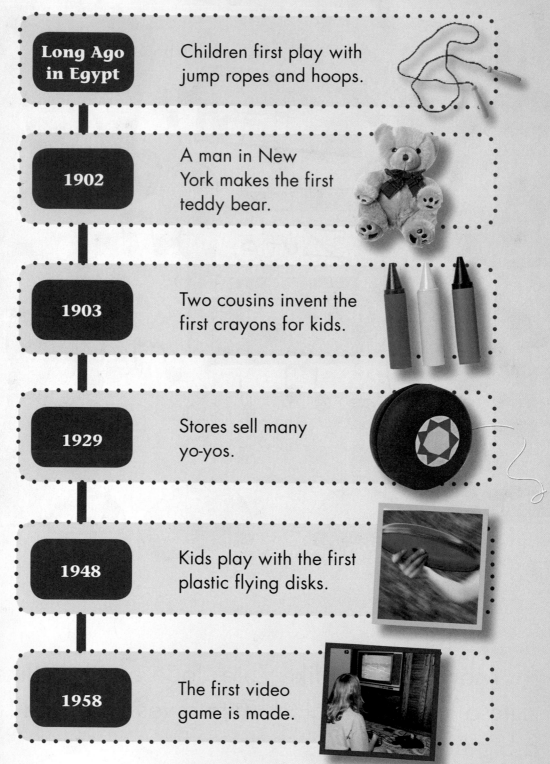

Long Ago in Egypt	Children first play with jump ropes and hoops.
1902	A man in New York makes the first teddy bear.
1903	Two cousins invent the first crayons for kids.
1929	Stores sell many yo-yos.
1948	Kids play with the first plastic flying disks.
1958	The first video game is made.

What new toy would you like to make?

My New Words

house*
A **house** is a building where people live.

idea*
An **idea** is a thought or plan.

invention
An **invention** is a new thing that someone thinks of and makes.

machine*
A **machine** is something with moving parts that does work for you.

sign*
A **sign** has pictures or words that tell you something important. A **sign** can also tell of something to come or something to look for.

*tested high-frequency words

Contents

WAYS TO COMMUNICATE

See page 53 for My New Words!

WAYS TO COMMUNICATE

Kids can communicate with pals in lots of ways. Kids can get together and chat. And they can chat when they are not close. Kids can use this machine to chat. Ring, ring!

Kids can use this machine to chat. One kid
hits his switch and chats. Then his buddy can
press her switch and chat back. Chatting like this
is fun! Would you like to try it?

Kids can communicate with notes. Kids can jot quick notes and hand them to pals.

Kids can send quick notes on machines too. Pals get these notes fast!

Kids can also send notes by adding stamps and dropping them in a box. Trucks pick up these notes. Planes can take notes and fly them to other lands. Have you found notes in your box?

Some kids must communicate with their hands. This kid made a sign with his hands that stood for "happy."

His buddy will use his hands and make signs back. These kids can have fun chatting this way.

Not just kids communicate. Hens cluck. Ducks quack. Some bugs can make songs by rubbing one back leg against another. Wild cats can hiss if they are mad. And when a puppy is happy, you can tell!

Dots
and
Dashes

by Aaron Lewis

What is a code? A code is a secret way to communicate. Codes can use letters, but not like you use them. Codes spell in quite an odd way. And codes can use things such as shapes and lines that stand for letters.

People can communicate with codes if they
know what those lines and shapes stand for.
Sending notes in code is like sending secrets.

This man is Samuel Morse. Samuel liked making codes. He made an odd code that used dots and dashes. These dots and dashes stood for letters.

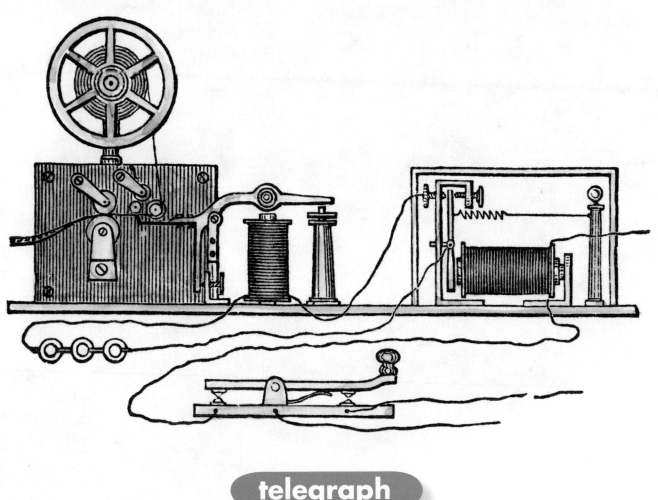

telegraph

This is a machine that Samuel made. He made it for sending his code. It had lots of switches and presses. It had long, skinny wires that rested against other long, skinny wires.

Samuel and his buddies tried sending notes by using his code. They tapped and tapped. They tapped long for dashes. They tapped fast for dots. Dash, dash, dot, dot, dash, dot, dot, dot.

Tap! Tap! Click! The code was sent through skinny wires to men miles and miles away. Click! Tap! Click!

These men jotted dots and dashes on note pads. They could tell what the dashes and dots stood for.

People in Samuel's time could not just chat with buddies miles and miles away. They could not send letters fast. Did Samuel's code help? Yes, it did.

A . _	S . . .
B _ . . .	T _
C _ . _ .	U . . _
D _ . .	V . . . _
E .	W . _ _
F . . _ .	X _ . . _
G _ _ .	Y _ . _ _
H	Z _ _ . .
I . .	1 . _ _ _ _
J . _ _ _	2 . . _ _ _
K _ . _	3 . . . _ _
L . _ . .	4 . . . . _
M _ _	5 . . . . .
N _ .	6 _ . . . .
O _ _ _	7 _ _ . . .
P . _ _ .	8 _ _ _ . .
Q _ _ . _	9 _ _ _ _ .
R . _ .	0 _ _ _ _ _

Samuel Morse had a wild idea that helped
people communicate. Samuel had found a way
to send notes fast by using a code. His code is
still used. It is named Morse code.

Gramps Learns New Things

by Roberto Marcos
illustrated by Elizabeth Allen

"Andy, Gramps is flying in to see us! He will get here by lunch," smiled Mom.

Andy grinned. Andy liked chatting with Gramps and telling him about his classes and his buddies.

At last Gramps rang the bell. He gave Mom and Andy big hugs. Mom smiled, "Andy misses you lots! It makes us happy when you are with us." "I bet Andy has lots to tell!" Gramps smiled.

Andy grinned. He did have lots to tell Gramps! Andy just got a computer. It stood on his desk against Mom's shelf in the den.

"My, that's a fancy one," said Gramps. "Look at those switches! Get my glasses. I will take a look."

"You can use this computer to send notes to buddies," said Andy.

"You can send notes with this?" asked Gramps.

"Yes," grinned Andy. "And then you can get notes back!"

"Why not try it?" smiled Andy.

Gramps tried and tried but could not send notes. At last Gramps cried, "I just can't use this silly thing!"

So Andy sat by Gramps and helped.

Gramps smiled and sent a note to his buddy.
"This is fun," smiled Gramps. "But can I use
this computer for other things?"

"You can use it to get on the Web. That's how
you can learn lots," Andy told him. "Let's try it."

Gramps found funny jokes and names of wild plants. He checked maps. "It is sunny and dry in this place!" said Gramps.

Gramps grinned. "It is fun to try new things. I learned lots from you, Andy. Thanks!"

When Gramps got home, he sent this note:

Andy, I got a computer. I used it and sent this note. This is fun, isn't it? I will like sending and getting notes!

Andy grinned. Now he and Gramps can chat all the time!

A to Z
in Sign Language

Aa Bb Cc Dd

Ee Ff Gg Hh

Ii Jj Kk Ll

Mm Nn Oo Pp

Qq Rr Ss Tt

Uu Vv Ww Xx

Yy Zz

Can you sign your name?

My New Words

against* The ladder is leaning **against** the wall.

communicate When you **communicate**, you share information or news.

computer A **computer** is a machine that can store and give information.

found* I **found** a dime.

letter A **letter** is a part of the alphabet.

secret If something is a **secret**, it is not known to everybody.

stood* We **stood** in line. The three letters **stood** for her name.

wild* When something is **wild**, it is not raised or grown by people.

*tested high-frequency words

Contents

What a Smart Idea!

See page 83 for My New Words!

What a Smart Idea!

This big spider is smart. It made a trap to get a snack. It mixed thick mud and silk to make its trap. Then it placed twigs and bits of bark on top. That made the trap hard to spot.

A fat frog hopped in front of the trap. It didn't spot the trap. The big spider jumped up and grabbed the frog.

Munch, munch! This frog will become a yummy snack.

This chimp likes bugs as snacks. But it's hard to get bugs. The chimp can try. But bugs hide in a big nest. And the chimp's arm just isn't long enough.

This chimp is smart. It picked up a long, sharp stick. It poked that stick far up in the nest. Bugs hopped on it and the chimp grabbed it back.

Munch, munch! These bugs will become a yummy snack.

A man thought fish would make a fine snack. But this man didn't have a pole. He didn't even have a stick. And the fish were swimming far from the dock. What if the man used a net?

The man picked up his big net and dipped it in the water. Six quick fish swam past. But one fish got stuck. The man grabbed his net and lifted it up. Munch, munch! This fish will become a yummy snack.

A kid went to an apple farm. She hoped to pick ripe, red apples as her snack. But they were far up in the top branches.

The kid thought long and hard. At last she grabbed a long stick and poked at the branches. Five big, ripe apples dropped. Munch, munch! These red apples will become a yummy snack.

A Nutty Story

by Consuela Sparks
illustrated by Laura Jacobsen

Crows are big, black birds. Crows can fly. Crows like to munch on things that come in shells, such as clams and nuts.

Are crows born smart? Can they even think or plan? Crows can't tell us. We must try to see.

People spotted crows dropping clams on rocks at the shore. But why? The clam shells cracked against hard rocks. The crows split those clam shells. Now the crows had clams to munch!

Crows must have thought this plan was good with nuts too. But nuts did not split. Crows came up with this new plan.

Lots of people stood as cars went past. A black crow sat on grass by them. It had six big nuts.

Cars went past. Horns honked. Tires spun. At last the cars stopped on the white line.

People crossed. The black crow grabbed nuts and made five short hops. Then it stopped. It didn't plan on crossing. It was fixing its lunch.

The crow dropped nuts in front of cars. Then it made five short hops back. Cars started up and went fast. While the crow sat on grass, cars drove on nuts and cracked them!

The crow hopped back when cars stopped again. It grabbed the cracked nuts that had become its lunch. Then it went on the grass and ate those nuts. Yum, yum! Crows ARE smart!

Think Smart!

by Carla Robbins
illustrated by Laura Freeman-Hines

School had ended. It was hot. Mark, Norm, and Barb sat on the shore. Fish swam back and forth in front of them.

"This is a bore," said Norm. "What can we do today?"

"Let's catch these big fish," said Barb. "If only we had fishing poles!"

"Let's use nets," stated Norm.

"What sort of idea is THAT?" asked Mark. "We don't even have nets."

"Well, we could make a thing that is LIKE a net," said Barb. "Let's think up lots of ideas and then form a plan."

"But Mark thinks my ideas are just silly!" Norm cried.

"Even plans that start silly can become smart," Barb stated.

"Let's list our ideas, starting with mine!" grinned Norm.

Barb smiled and got her note pad.

Norm said, "Let's catch fish with Mom's scarf."
Barb added, "Let's catch fish with sharp twigs."
Barb jotted lots of ideas. Then she stopped.
"These ideas are not bad," Barb said, "but we
must think of more."

Mark asked if hats with big brims could catch
fish. The kids thought. Then Mark cried, "I know
a plan to try!"

Mark grabbed the hat that Barb had on.

He used the string to put Barb's hat on a branch. Mark had made this thing to catch fish! It had a pole. It was LIKE a net. The kids went fishing.

A big fish swam by. Barb tugged on the branch and lifted her big hat. She had the fish!

Then Norm and Mark got more fish. Soon six big fish flopped on shore.

"Let's take them home and ask Mom to bake them for lunch," stated Barb.

Mark, Norm, and Barb ate yummy fish in their yard.

"Mark's plan was smart," grinned Barb.

"It wasn't just my plan," stated Mark. "Your ideas helped me think up that smart plan."

"They did?" smiled Barb.

Mark smiled back. "Your ideas made ME start thinking!"

I Built a Fabulous Machine

by Jack Prelutsky

Read Together

I built a fabulous machine
to keep my room completely clean.
It swept it up in nothing flat—
has anybody seen the cat?

My New Words

become*   It has **become** warmer.

brim   A **brim** is a wide edge that sticks out from around a hat.

crow   A **crow** is a large, shiny, black bird with a loud cry.

even*   **Even** though it was hot, she wore a jacket. Do you **even** know that boy you waved to?

front*   The **front** part of something is the part that faces forward. The **front** of something is also the first part or the beginning.

spider   A **spider** is very small and has eight legs.

thought*   A **thought** is something that a person thinks.

*tested high-frequency words

Contents

Figure It Out

See page 113 for My New Words!

Figure It Out

Can kids think smart? Kids can.

At home, some things are hard to get to. This kid can't get to the sink. What can kids do about this problem?

Kids can just step up. But it's easy to slip. Kids must hang on as they step up and step down.

These kids will have a party. Kids will invite their pals. Kids make cards that tell the time and place of the party. Kids make maps on the cards and write, "Follow this map for fun!"

It is time to send the cards. But these kids have a problem. They do not have stamps.

As usual, these kids think smart. These kids will TAKE the cards to their pals!

Pet dogs must get fed and brushed. They must go out too. But big dogs can tug hard and escape. If that happens, it's a big problem!

This kid knew that it takes more than one kid to take a huge dog out. He asked his pal for help. If the dog tugs hard, both kids just tug back. This dog can't run off!

Can kids think smart? Kids can!

Justin's Bikes for Kids

by Becca Case
illustrated by Joel Spector

Justin liked riding racing bikes. He also liked fixing them.

Justin spotted an old bike. He fixed it up like new. Fixing bikes was easy and fun for Justin.

Justin rode his fixed-up bike. It was not a racing bike. Justin didn't like it as much as the usual racing bike he rode.

Then he fixed up one more bike. Justin still liked his racing bike more. But he DID like fixing bikes! This gave Justin an idea.

Justin knew a place to take his fixed-up bikes. Kids who did not have moms or dads lived at this place. Justin gave these kids his bikes.

The kids liked Justin's bikes. They rode them and did tricks on them. This made Justin excited. But that place had lots more kids!

Justin wanted to follow the same plan. Justin would fix up more bikes for these kids as well.

Justin had to fix lots of bikes. But it was hard to get that many old bikes. Then lots of people started to give Justin bikes to fix.

Justin gave a bike to every kid at that place!
Then Justin made bikes for lots more kids at lots
more places. His bikes made lots of kids happy.
Making kids happy made Justin happy too.

The Huge TURNiP

by Therese Evans
illustrated by Jackie Urbanovic

One morning, Pops Popkins spotted a big,
white seed in his yard. He picked it up.

"This isn't a usual seed," stated Pops. "It
has odd patches on it. I think I will plant it in
my garden."

Next morning, Pops checked his garden. That
seed had become a huge turnip plant.

"This will last us a long, long time," he cried.
"I must harvest it."

Pops started tugging hard, but the plant was stuck. He tugged and tugged, but that turnip was still stuck. At last his hands got sore.

He ran up on his porch and yelled, "Help!" Gram came out.

"Follow me!" cried Pops. Then he led Gram to his garden. Together they tugged and tugged. That plant was still stuck.

"More help!" yelled Pops.

His kid ran up and helped them tug. But that turnip was still stuck.

"More help!" yelled Pops.

His puppy and kitten came running. They tugged and tugged. But that huge turnip was still stuck.

At last they gave up.
"Forget it. It's just no use," said Pops.

Then five mice popped up. "Let us tug!"

"Mice can't get this turnip up if we can't," said Pops.

"But what if we all tug?" asked the five mice. "That will make it easy."

Pops grabbed the turnip. Gram grabbed Pops. The kid grabbed Gram's belt. The puppy and kitten grabbed the kid's arms. And all five mice grabbed the puppy and kitten.

POP! Up came that huge turnip at last.

Next morning, Pops made turnip muffins.
His kid mashed and fried turnips. Gram baked
turnip cake.

Gram piled yummy turnip things on plates.
Then they ate and ate and ate!

Pops smiled, "I knew it was not a usual seed."

Pet Puzzle

Read Together

Three children have different pets. Read the clues.
Can you figure out who has which pet?

Ana's pet does not meow.
Ana's pet likes bones.

Lin's pet does not swim.
Lin's pet does not bark.

Tom's pet does not bark.
Tom's pet does not meow.

Answers: Ana has a dog. Lin has a cat. Tom has a fish.

112

My New Words

easy*   If something is **easy**, it is not hard to do or understand.

follow*   When you **follow** someone or something, you go after that person or thing.

harvest   When you **harvest**, you gather in the crops and store them.

knew*   I **knew** the answer.

seed   A **seed** is the part of a plant that grows into a new plant.

turnip   A **turnip** is the large, round root of a garden plant. It is eaten as a vegetable.

usual*   If something is **usual**, it is often seen, or it often happens.

*tested high-frequency words

Contents

Where Ideas Come From

See page 143 for My New Words!

Where Ideas Come From

Where can kids get smart ideas? It's easy! Kids can click buttons or flip pages! Kids can think hard.

Would you like to tell funny jokes or plant nice gardens? Would you like to write silly, sad, or happy tales?

Click buttons! Flip pages! Think, think, think! You'll get plenty of fine ideas.

A smart idea can start with just a guess. Then it gets tested to tell if it is correct or not.

If a guess isn't correct, that's OK. Tests help us. They make us think about what to try next.

Smart ideas can take lots of testing. That can take time, but it'll let us end up with smart answers!

Fun Party Ideas
1. tag
2. egg toss
3. make crafts
4. sing
5. share cake
6. water balloons
7. give gifts

Kids can help kids get ideas. Take time to trade ideas with a pal. You'll both think up lots of fun things. Make a nice, long list. Pick the best things and try them.

It's fine to get ideas from artists. Just don't forget to invent your art ideas too.

Artists use colors, along with shapes, in art. When you admire art, think about its colors and shapes. You can get the best ideas. Just think!

Beautiful IDEAS

by Josie Abrams

Fine artists get ideas for art in many places. Artist Mary Cassatt didn't have kids, but she got along well with them.

Children on the Beach, 1884, Mary Cassatt.

Spending time with both kids and moms helped her get ideas for her art.

In Mary Cassatt's art, moms hug kids. Girls sit by the shore, and kids run in gardens.

Claude Monet had huge gardens filled with bursts of color. This artist liked standing and gazing at his fine gardens.

The Japanese Bridge, Giverny, 1892, Claude Monet.

Can you guess where Claude Monet got ideas for his art? Yes! When you see his art, you'll think that you are standing in his fine garden with him.

When artist Rufino Tamayo was a kid, he helped sell fresh plums and limes. He helped sell fresh corn, garlic, and peppers too.

Still Life of Watermelon and Plums, 1941, Rufino Tamayo.

Later, Rufino Tamayo made pictures of these yummy things in his art.

This artist used his brush to make swirls and curls of color that shimmer and shine.

Clementine Hunter didn't make her first art until she was past fifty. Things around her gave her ideas. She put gardens and churches in her art.

The Wash, 1950s, Clementine Hunter.

With her brush, she made long, dirt paths.
She made shirts drying on lines.

Clementine Hunter kept making art until she
was quite old.

YELP! HELP!

by Gloria Vallejo
illustrated by Rémy Simard

Flash! Curtis saw a short, odd girl enter his home. She wore dirty red socks and had curls the color of grass.

"I'm Yelp, the Help Elf," stated the girl.
"Help Elf?" asked Curtis.
"Yes, sir," said Yelp. "I help. That's what a
Help Elf does best."

"In that case, can you help make my lunch?"
Curtis asked.

Yelp clapped her hands twice. Then she
handed Curtis a card filled with notes.

"Crackers with butter and jam," Curtis read.
"That's not bad. Let's try it." But when Curtis
turned, he didn't spot Yelp.

After class, both tires on Curtis's bike were
flat. "Yelp! Help!" Curtis cried.

Along came Yelp. She clapped her hands
twice, and a pump landed next to Curtis.

Then Curtis pumped up his tires.
Curtis had to admit that Yelp's pump
helped. "But I'm the one who fixed those tires,"
Curtis thought.

At home, Curtis set his pack on his desk.
"Yelp! Help!" yelled Curtis. "I must make up a
tale that's five chapters long. And I'm stuck on
the first page."

Yelp dropped a fat pencil on Curtis's desk.
"This is filled with ideas," said Yelp. "It'll help."
"I guess that's as much help as I'll get," Curtis
said as Yelp slid under the bed.

Yelp kept popping in and out of Curtis's life.
Curtis asked for help with a test. Yelp gave
him pages of notes.

Curtis asked for help making gifts for pals.
Yelp gave him five pictures as ideas.

At last, Yelp stated, "My time here is up, Mister. I'm glad I helped."

"Helped?" cried Curtis. "I'm the one who did these things! You just came up with ideas!"

"Then I did my job well," stated Yelp. "You had to learn that ideas are just the start. Hard work matters just as much."

Then—

Flash! Yelp went away for good!

Meet
Scott Gustafson
Book Illustrator

My name is Scott Gustafson. I draw pictures for kids' books. I get my ideas from many places. Sometimes I remember a game I played as a child. I even get ideas while walking my dog! But books are my favorite source. I get a lot of ideas when I go to libraries.

My New Words

admire　When you **admire** something, you look at it with pleasure.

along*　Trees are planted **along** the street.
We took our dog **along**.
I get **along** well with him.

artist　An **artist** is a person who makes art.

both*　**Both** houses are pink.
Both belong to her.

color*　A **color** is either red, yellow, blue, or any of these mixed together.

elf　In stories, an **elf** is a tiny make-believe person.

guess*　A **guess** is an idea you have when you are not sure of something.

plenty　**Plenty** is all that you need.
You have **plenty** of time.

*tested high-frequency words

Acknowledgments

Text

Every effort has been made to locate the copyright owner of material reproduced in this component. Omissions brought to our attention will be corrected in subsequent editions. Grateful acknowledgment is made to the following for copyrighted material.

82 HarperCollins "I Built a Fabulous Machine" by Jack Prelutsky from *It's Raining Pigs And Noodles*. Text copyright © 2000 by Jack Prelutsky. Used by permission of HarperCollins Publishers.

Illustrations

Cover: Jeff Shelly, Rémy Simard; **4, 5, 18–25** Bill McGuire; **29, 44–51** Elizabeth Allen; **55, 70–81** Laura Freeman-Hines; **55, 64–69** Laura Jacobsen; **82** Jeff Shelly; **84, 85, 92–99** Joel Spector; **86–91** Gary LaCoste; **100–111** Jackie Urbanovic; **115, 130–141** Rémy Simard.

Photographs

Every effort has been made to secure permission and provide appropriate credit for photographic material. The publisher deeply regrets any omission and pledges to correct errors called to its attention in subsequent editions.

Unless otherwise acknowledged, all photographs are the property of Pearson Education, Inc.

Photo locators denoted as follows: Top (T), Center (C), Bottom (B), Left (L), Right (R), Background (Bkgd)

1 (C) Blend Images/Getty Images; **3** (TC) ©Lindsey Stock/DK Images, (BR) Corbis, (T) DK Images; **6** (CL) ©Akhtar Soomro/Corbis, (T) ©Bettmann/Corbis; **7** (CR) ©Lindsey Stock/DK Images, (T) Corbis, (CL) DK Images; **8** (T) DK Images; **9** (T) ©ImageState; **12** (CR) ©Myrleen Ferguson Cate/PhotoEdit, (CL) ©William Sallaz/Duomo/Corbis; **14** (CR, CL) ©Rollerblade USA Corp.; **15** (C) ©Charlie Borland/Index Open; **16** (T) ©Charlie Borland/Index Open; **17** (T) ©Lori Adamski Peek/Getty Images; **26** (CR) ©Andy Crawford/DK Images, (T) ©Dave King/DK Images, (BR) ©FogStock/Index Open, (TR) ©photolibrary/Index Open, (CR) DK Images; **28** (C) Blend Images/Getty Images; **30** (C) Getty Images; **31** (C) ©Tony Freeman/PhotoEdit; **32** (CR) Blend Images/Getty Images; **33** (C) ©Tony Freeman/PhotoEdit; **35** (C) ©Myrleen Ferguson Cate/PhotoEdit; **38** (C) The Granger Collection, NY; **39** (C) North Wind Picture Archives; **40** (T) The Granger Collection, NY; **41** (T) North Wind Picture Archives; **42** (C) North Wind Picture Archives; **56** (TC) ©Anthony Bannister/Corbis; **57** (TC) Getty Images; **58** (TC) Getty Images; **59** (T) ©Steve Bloom Images/Alamy Images; **60** (I) ©Dennis Frates/Alamy Images; **61** (T) ©Colinspics/Alamy Images; **62** (TC) ©James Lauritz/Alamy Images; **63** (TC) ©Michael Newman/PhotoEdit; **64** (TL) Getty Images; **66** (BR) Getty Images; **69** (BL) Getty Images; **85** (BR) ©Pat Doyle/Corbis; **112** (TR, BR) ©Pat Doyle/Corbis, (CR) ©Royalty-Free/Corbis; **114** (C) Juan Silva/Getty Images; **117** (C) ©Michael Goldman/Getty Images; **118** (C) ©Richard T. Nowitz; **121** (CL) ©Royalty-Free/Corbis, (TC) Juan Silva/Getty Images; **122** (C) ©Bettmann/Corbis, (CL) Culver Pictures Inc.; **123** (C) ©Mary Cassatt (1845-1926/American) oil on canvas, National Gallery of Art, Washington, D.C./age fotostock/SuperStock, (C) Getty Images; **124** (CL, C) ©Musee Marmottan, Paris, France/Giraudon/Bridgeman Art Library; **125** (C) The Japanese Bridge, Giverny, 1892 (oil on canvas), Claude Monet/©Private Collection/Bridgeman Art Library; **126** (CR) ©Hulton-Deutsch Collection/Corbis, (CL) ©Thinkstock; **127** (C) ©Christie's Images/Bridgeman Art Library, (TC) Getty Images; **128** (CL) ©age fotostock/SuperStock, (CR) Courtesy of the Cammie G. Henry Research Center, Watson Memorial Libary, Northwestern State University of Louisiana; **129** (TC) Getty Images, (C) The Wash 1950s, painting by Clementine Hunter. Oil on board, 18 by 24 in. The Ethel Morrison Van Derlip Fund/The Minneapolis Institute of Arts.